Intro to Hmong

Bela Davis

Hmoob

Abdo Kids Junior
is an Imprint of Abdo Kids
abdobooks.com

abdobooks.com

Published by Abdo Kids, a division of ABDO, P.O. Box 398166, Minneapolis, Minnesota 55439.
Copyright © 2025 by Abdo Consulting Group, Inc. International copyrights reserved in all countries. No part of this book may be reproduced in any form without written permission from the publisher.
Abdo Kids Junior™ is a trademark and logo of Abdo Kids.

Printed in the United States of America, North Mankato, Minnesota.

102024

012025

Consultant: Pakou Moua

Photo Credits: Getty Images, Shutterstock

Production Contributors: Teddy Borth, Jennie Forsberg, Grace Hansen

Design Contributors: Candice Keimig, Colleen McLaren

Library of Congress Control Number: 2024936628

Publisher's Cataloging-in-Publication Data

Names: Davis, Bela, author.

Title: Intro to Hmong / by Bela Davis

Description: Minneapolis, Minnesota : Abdo Kids, 2025 | Series: Intro to language set 2 | Includes online resources and index.

Identifiers: ISBN 9798384902843 (lib. bdg.) | ISBN 9798384903543 (ebook) | ISBN 9798384903895 (Read-to-me ebook)

Subjects: LCSH: Informal language learning--Juvenile literature. | Language and languages--Juvenile literature. | Bilingual books--Juvenile literature. | Language acquisition--Juvenile literature.

Classification: DDC 418--dc23

Table of Contents

Intro to Hmong

Hmong is spoken around the world. Let's learn some words!

China
Myanmar
Laos
Thailand
Vietnam
Asia
N
W
E
S
Hmong is an official language

ib
(ee)
one

ob
(ah)
two

rau
(jow)
six

xya
(see•ah)
seven

peb
(bay)
three

plaub
(blau)
four

tsib
(jee)
five

yim
(yee)
eight

cuaj
(kyo•ah)
nine

kaum
(gau)
ten

kaum ib

(gau ee)

eleven

kaum ob

(gau ah)

twelve

kaum rau

(gau jow)

sixteen

kaum xya

(gau see•ah)

seventeen

kaum peb
(gau bay)
thirteen

kaum plaub
(gau blau)
fourteen

kaum tsib
(gau jee)
fifteen

kaum yim
(gau yee)
eighteen

kaum cuaj
(gau kyo•ah)
nineteen

nees kaum
(neng gau)
twenty

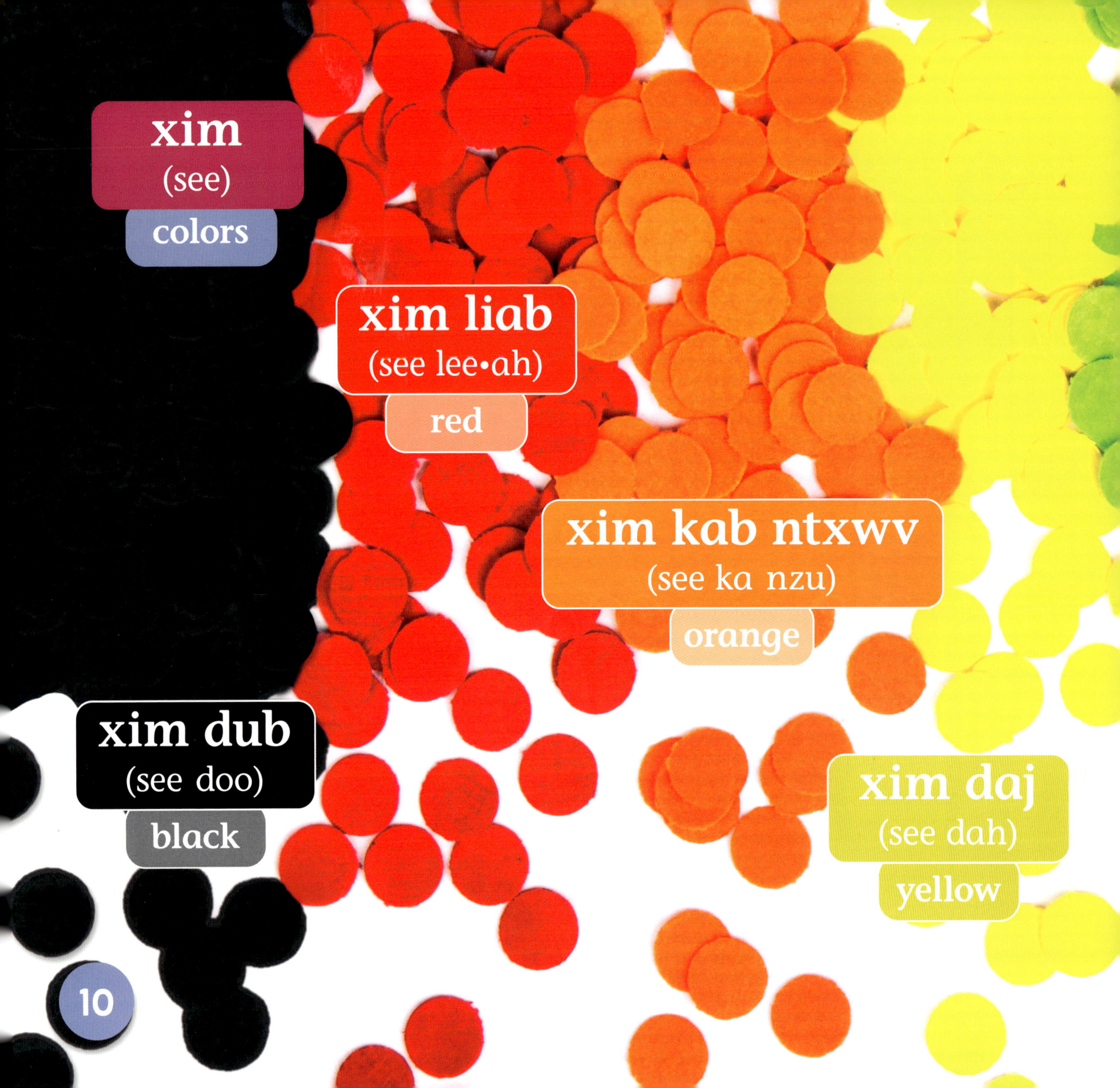
xim
(see)
colors
xim liab
(see lee•ah)
red
xim kab ntxwv
(see ka nzu)
orange
xim dub
(see doo)
black
xim daj
(see dah)
yellow

xim ntsuab
(see ju•ah)
green
xim xiav
(see see•ah)
blue
xim dawb
(see dargh)
white
xim paj ntshav
(see pa ncha)
purple

nyob zoo
(nyah shawng)
hello

sib ntsib dua
(see jee doo•ah)
goodbye

nyob zoo sawv ntxov
(nyah shawng sarg dzaow)
good morning

nyob zoo hmo ntuj
(nyah shawng hmoh ntoo)
good night

thov
(taw)
please

ua tsaug
(oo jau)
thank you

yog
(yaw)
yes

tsis yog
(jee yaw)
no

tsev neeg
(cheh neng)
family

niam
(neh•yah)
mother

txiv
(zee)
father

niam laus
(neh•yah laow)
older sister

tij laug
(tee laow)
older brother

niam hluas
(neh•yah hloo•wah)
younger sister

kwv
(kuh)
younger brother

niam tais
(ney•ah tai)
mother's mother

yawm txiv
(yargh za•ee)
mother's father

pog
(paw)
father's mother

yawg
(yargh)
father's father

tsiaj
(jey•ah)
animals
aub
(ow)
dog
miv
(mee)
cat

noog
(nong)
bird
ntses
(jaw•eh)
fish

chaw (chah) – Places

tsev
(jeh)
house

tsev kawm ntawv
(jeh kargh ntargh)
school

chaw ua si
(chah oo•wah see)
park

ntug dej hiav txwv
(ntoo deh he•yah zuh)
beach

Reading Hmong

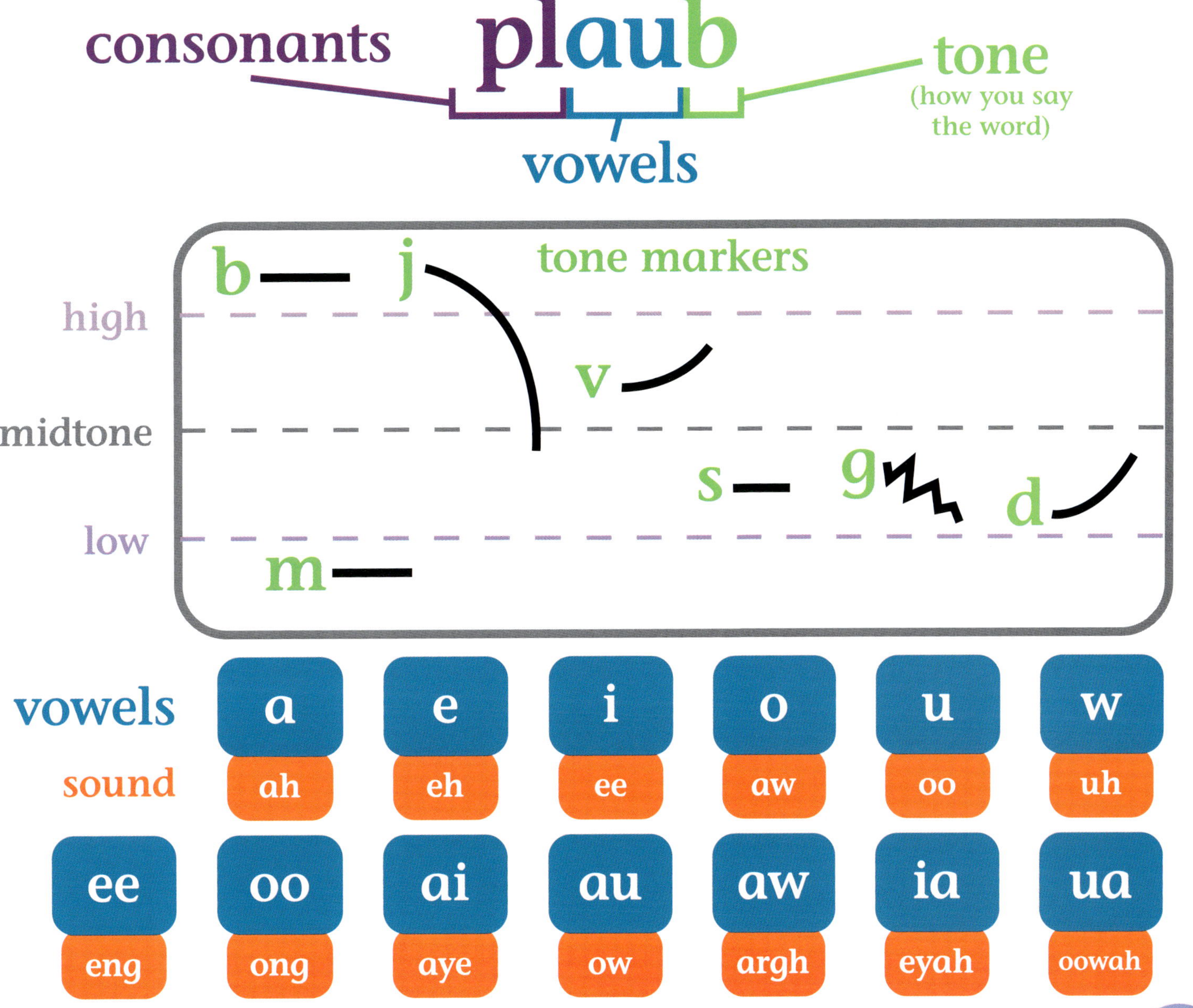

Index

Visit **abdokids.com** to access crafts, games, videos, and more!

Use Abdo Kids code

IIK2843

or scan this QR code!